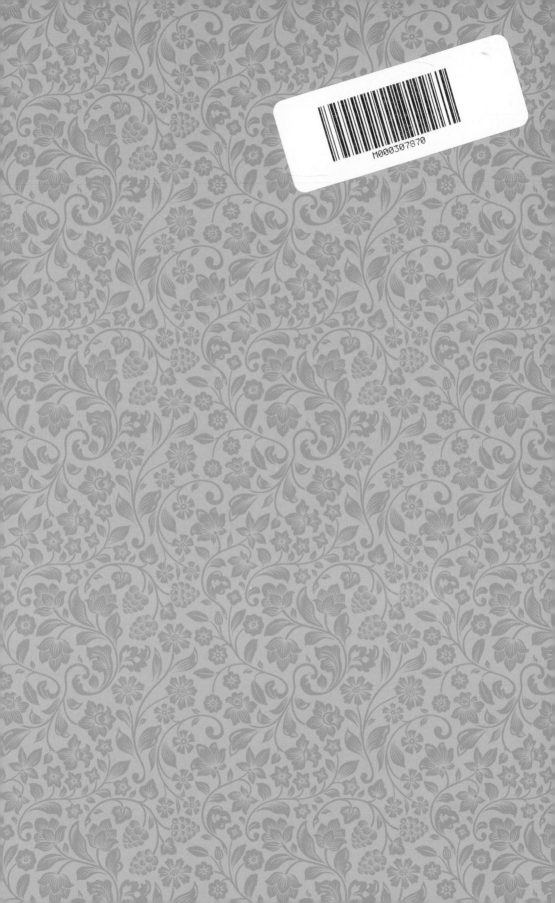

This book belongs to

OLA HES ♥

AUTUMN
PUBLISHING

Published in 2021
First published in the UK by Autumn Publishing
An imprint of Igloo Books Ltd
Cottage Farm, NN6 0BJ, UK
Owned by Bonnier Books
Sveavägen 56, Stockholm, Sweden

www.autumnpublishing.co.uk

1121 001
2 4 6 8 10 9 7 5 3 1
ISBN 978-1-80108-237-2

Wildlife consultancy by David Winnard

Illustrated by Amelia Herbertson
Written by Suzanne Fossey

Designed by Chris Stanley
Edited by Suzanne Fossey

The publisher would like to thank Claire Sipi for
proofreading and Elizabeth Wise for the index.

Printed and manufactured in China.

All instructions contained within should be followed carefully and
accurately and the Publisher cannot accept any liability for injury, loss
or damage to any user or property following suggestions in this book.
Children should always be accompanied by a responsible adult, and
it is the responsibility of every user of this book to assess individual
circumstances and potential dangers of any activity they wish to
undertake. Be aware of local laws, especially those regarding entry
and trespass, and those regarding collection of wild materials including
feathers, plants and seeds. This book is for entertainment purposes only.
Plants, fungi and berries may be poisonous so should be double-checked
for accuracy and are collected at the reader's own risk.

How to Find a
Fairy

AUTUMN
PUBLISHING

Contents

The Start of Something Magical...   6
The Fairy Finder's Charter   8
A Fairy Finder's Kit   9
A Finder's Journal   10

The Return of Spring   12

The First Flowers of Spring   14
Eggciting Seed Pots   16
The Importance of Bees   18
Bumblebee, Honeybee or Wasp?   19
Exploring Your Garden Pond   20
Feather by Feather   22
Ready for Nesting   24
Welcome, Feathered Friends   25

Sun-kissed Summer Days   26

Garden Trees   28
Night Blooming Flowers   30
How Seeds Grow   32
Are There Bats in Your Garden?   34
The Fairy Postal Express   36
Fairy Song Catchers   38

The Golden Glow of Autumn········ 40

Beautiful Butterflies ············· 42
Scavenger Hunt ··········· 44
Common Garden Fruits ········· 46
Six Ways to Help Butterflies
     and Moths in Autumn ········· 48
A Moth's Midnight Feast ········· 49
Night Fliers ··········· 50
Wonderful Wormery ·········· 52
Following Footprints ········· 54
The World of Minibeasts ········· 56

Winter Winds ··········· 58

Winter Wildlife Sanctuaries ········· 60
Bug Hotels ········· 62
Hidden Corners ········· 64
Light the Way ········· 66
Winter Berries ········· 68
Send a Magical Invitation ········· 70

A Finder's Notebook········· 72
Index ········· 96

The Start of Something Magical...

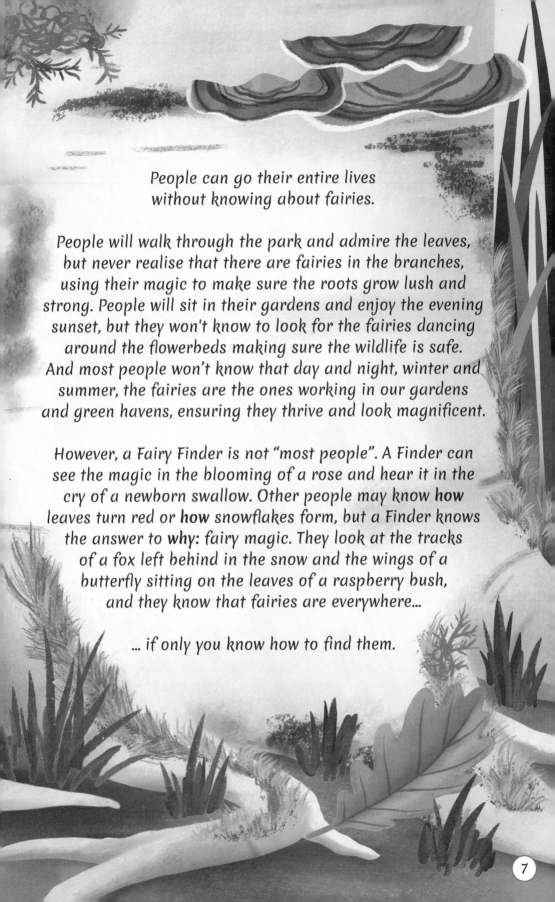

People can go their entire lives
without knowing about fairies.

People will walk through the park and admire the leaves,
but never realise that there are fairies in the branches,
using their magic to make sure the roots grow lush and
strong. People will sit in their gardens and enjoy the evening
sunset, but they won't know to look for the fairies dancing
around the flowerbeds making sure the wildlife is safe.
And most people won't know that day and night, winter and
summer, the fairies are the ones working in our gardens
and green havens, ensuring they thrive and look magnificent.

However, a Fairy Finder is not "most people". A Finder can
see the magic in the blooming of a rose and hear it in the
cry of a newborn swallow. Other people may know **how**
leaves turn red or **how** snowflakes form, but a Finder knows
the answer to **why**: fairy magic. They look at the tracks
of a fox left behind in the snow and the wings of a
butterfly sitting on the leaves of a raspberry bush,
and they know that fairies are everywhere...

... if only you know how to find them.

The Fairy Finder's Charter

The Charter governs how a Fairy Finder carries out their sacred duty. These rules explain how to look after these magical creatures. You should put them into practice every time you step outside.

· Never eat anything you find outdoors unless an expert has said it's safe. Experts include: adults and the Fairy Finder leader, Lady Zinnia Moonspider.

· Always make sure an adult knows what you're doing and where you are. Finders never go off without telling someone.

· Be careful especially near deep water, in new places or when outside at night. Finders are careful explorers.

· Finders must get permission to pick flowers or plants, and should only take flowers that there are a lot of.

· It is not becoming of a Finder to trespass on property that they do have permission to be on. Always ask first.

· Finders must make sure to put things back and never leave any litter.

· Above all, Fairy Finders must agree to protect wildlife and fairies, and look after their gardens.

A Fairy Finder's Kit

Fairies are shy, quiet creatures who keep to themselves. If you're going to find them, you will need some special fairy-finding equipment.

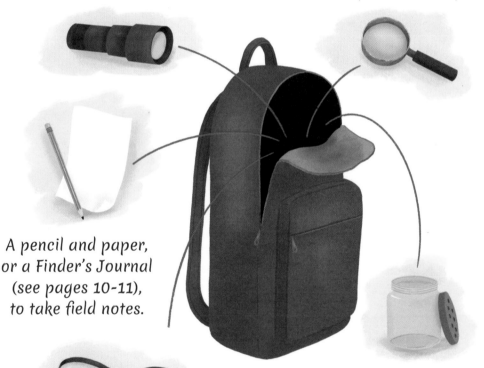

A torch, for night-time exploring.

A magnifying glass, because fairy footprints are tiny.

A pencil and paper, or a Finder's Journal (see pages 10-11), to take field notes.

A small jar or a bug box, so that you can have a closer look at the things you find. Just remember to be gentle and put them back where you found them.

A pair of binoculars can be helpful.

A Finder's Journal

Now that you've decided to become a Fairy Finder, you will need a journal so that you can record your observations. Most Finders make their own journals using found objects, such as feathers and leaves. No two journals are the same.

1 Find some thick paper and rub it all over with a wet teabag to make it look old. Allow one side to dry before staining the other.

2 Fold the paper in half and tie a string around the fold. You can add a cardboard cover if you like.

3 Look around your garden for feathers, acorns or leaves and tie them together and attach them to that they hang off the bottom of your book for decoration. These found objects let other Finders know you're one of them.

4 Stick dry leaves and flowers on the pages of your journal. You can make them last longer by coating them with clear nail varnish before you glue them in. Make sure they're dry first.

5 Make some berry ink to record your notes. Gather a handful of raspberries or blackberries. Put the berries into a saucepan with half a teaspoon of vinegar and half a teaspoon of salt. Ask an adult to help you boil the ingredients for a few minutes. When the mixture has cooled down, sieve it into a small bowl or jar. Use a paintbrush or quill to start writing.

6 Use your notebook to write about all the fairy magic you've seen in your garden. That way, if you do meet another Finder, you can compare notes!

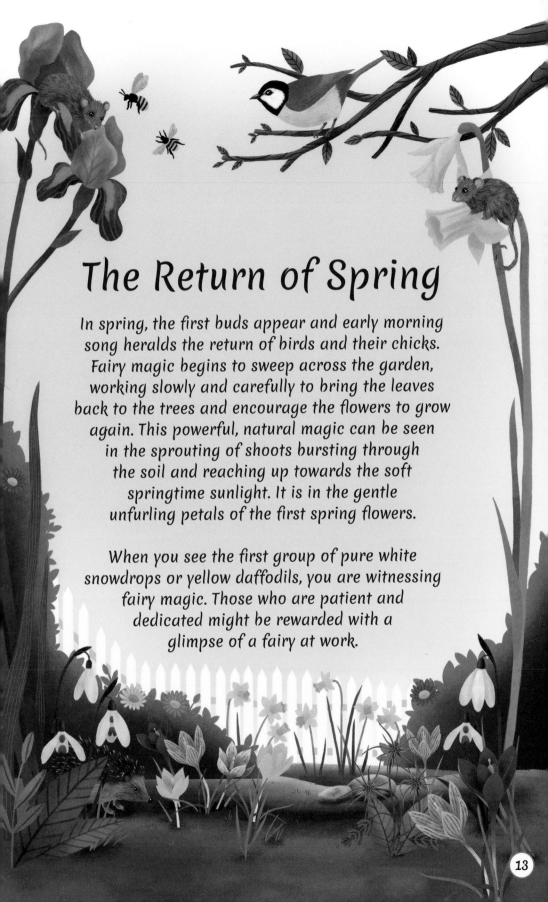

The Return of Spring

In spring, the first buds appear and early morning
song heralds the return of birds and their chicks.
Fairy magic begins to sweep across the garden,
working slowly and carefully to bring the leaves
back to the trees and encourage the flowers to grow
again. This powerful, natural magic can be seen
in the sprouting of shoots bursting through
the soil and reaching up towards the soft
springtime sunlight. It is in the gentle
unfurling petals of the first spring flowers.

When you see the first group of pure white
snowdrops or yellow daffodils, you are witnessing
fairy magic. Those who are patient and
dedicated might be rewarded with a
glimpse of a fairy at work.

The First Flowers of Spring

One of the best things about winter giving way to spring is the beautiful parade of colour that appears when flowers bloom. The fairies work very hard to make the garden look as bright and colourful as they can.

Snowdrops

These delicate, pure white flowers are a favourite of the fairies, and they're often the first flowers to bloom in spring. Their thin stems will push up through any snow still lingering on the ground.

Crocuses

The riotous colours of crocuses stand out against the browns and greys of a spring garden. They are loved by bees and by fairies, who, in early spring, like to fall asleep inside the tall cup-shaped petals.

Daffodils

No flower marks the true start of spring better than the daffodil, with their bright yellow petals and trumpet-shaped middles. Groups of daffodils are a symbol of friendship, and fairies love to dance through them.

Irises

Named after the Greek goddess of the rainbow, the iris flower can bloom in almost any colour. Its elegant, wavy, lace-like petals are very attractive to fairies, who use them for clothing and decoration.

FAIRY FAVOURITE:
Cloudy Starwort

This very rare flower is found only in gardens that are home to a fairy King or Queen. Its thin orange and purple petals are a distinctive star shape, and its smell is often said to be like spiced hot chocolate.

Eggciting Seed Pots

Because fairies are so busy looking after everything in your garden, it will make them really happy if you help them with a few things. In fact, they'd be delighted if you grew new plants from seeds, ready for planting later in the summer.

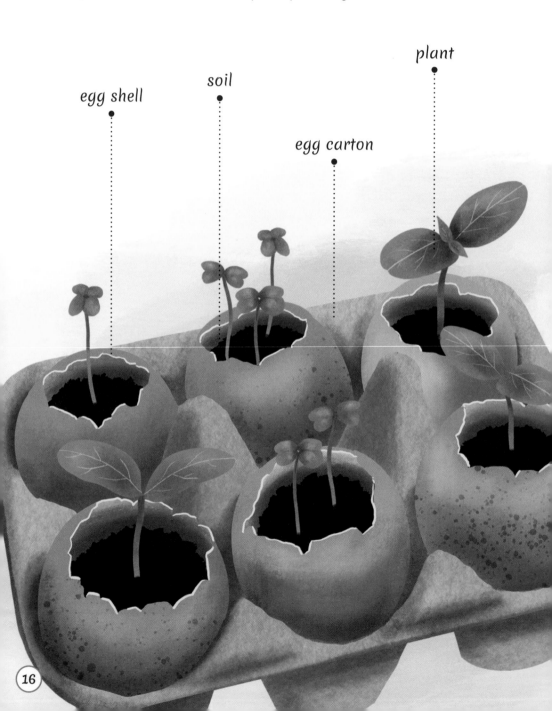

egg shell

soil

egg carton

plant

You will need: • hard-boiled eggs • an egg carton • soil
• a saucepan • water • seeds • a needle • an adult to help

1

Cool the eggs in a bowl of cold water. Then carefully crack open the tops and spoon out the insides. (They're great in sandwiches!)

2

Ask an adult to help boil the empty shells once more to remove traces of egg. Don't pour the water away! You'll need it for step 6.

3

Dry the shells and carefully pierce the bottom of each one with a needle. Ask an adult to help you.

4

Put the eggshells in the egg carton and partially fill each shell with soil.

5

Plant a few of your chosen seeds in each shell and then cover the seeds with some more soil.

6

Use the water from step 2 to water your seedlings, but make sure it has cooled down first!

7

Once the seedlings have sprouted, plant the entire shell in a larger pot or in your garden, and watch your seedlings flourish!

The Importance of Bees

You may have seen bumblebees buzzing around your garden, but did you know that they are very important? They help humans grow food and they help fairies spread beautiful flowers through a process called pollination.

Bumblebees stop at flowers to drink the sweet nectar, which gives them energy. They also collect a yellow dust called pollen and store it in baskets on their back legs. Once they've finished at one flower, they move onto the next, where some of the pollen they have collected falls off. The flower uses this pollen to help make seeds. A few months later, the seeds germinate and grow into new flowers. A bumblebee will visit the new flower and the cycle starts all over again.

Fairies sing to attract bees. So if you see a bee buzzing around a flowers, listen really closely, because you might just hear a sweet fairy melody.

If you see exhausted-looking bees in your garden, don't leave out sugar or honey water, as it's not good for them. A dish of water is more helpful. Fill it with pebbles for the bees to rest on.

Bumblebee, Honeybee or Wasp?

All three will most likely visit your garden at one point during the year, so can you tell a bumblebee from a honeybee or wasp?

Bumblebee

Big, round and fuzzy

Striped black, white and golden orange

Visits flowers to collect pollen and nectar

Legs are hidden when flying

Only stings when provoked

Honeybee

Thin, with few hairs

Striped black and yellow

Visits flowers to collect pollen and nectar

Legs hang down when flying

Only stings when provoked

Wasp

Thin, with very few or no hairs

Striped with very bright yellow and black

Flies around any food and drink left outside

Legs hang down when flying

Can be aggressive and ready to sting

Exploring Your Garden Pond

Ponds provide water to thirsty birds and mammals, as well as a place for fairies to bathe. They are also home to some amazing creatures you won't see elsewhere. Sit near a pond and see how many of these creatures you can spot.

Four-Spotted Chaser

This brown dragonfly is usually seen hovering around ponds during June. It eats mosquitoes, gnats and midges, and gets its name from the black spot on each of its four wings.

Common Blue Damselfly

This bright blue damselfly is common around ponds and it has long wings and black stripes across its body. When the damselfly first emerges from an egg, its body is a pink-brown colour. After a few days, the damselfly turns a vibrant blue.

Backswimmer

This brown insect has reddish eyes and oar-like legs, and it swims around on its back. The backswimmer searches the pond for other insects, tadpoles and small fish to eat. Don't handle these insects as they have toxic saliva and their bite can be painful!

Pond Skater

This brownish-black, long-legged insect has tiny water-repellent hairs on the bottom of its feet, allowing it to "skate" across the water without sinking. It feeds on other insects by detecting vibrations on the surface of the water.

Pond Snail

The pond snail is about three times larger than a garden snail, and has a fragile, brown-yellow pointed shell. It likes to stay in ponds with lots of plants for it to eat.

Duckweed

The small green leaves of the duckweed plant float on top of the water, forming a "carpet" across the surface. It can double in size within two to three days and will quickly cover a pond if it's not cleared, or eaten by animals.

Tadpoles

Tadpoles have round heads and long, flat tails. They swim under the water, eating algae and plants. As they grow up, they sprout legs and their bodies and heads completely change shape, until they become frogs, toads or newts.

Feather by Feather

Birds visit your garden for a rest, some food, or to have a talk with the fairies. Being able to identify which birds have stopped by is a Finder skill worth learning.

House Sparrow

These little birds have full chests, round heads and short tails. Their wings are covered in black and brown striped feathers. They can be seen in city streets, in parks and gardens, often fluttering down to peck at crumbs. Sparrows live in groups called hosts.

Barn Swallow

These nimble fliers have steely-blue bodies, white chests and red faces. Their long wings and forked tails help them perform quick turns in the air, to catch insects mid-flight. A group of swallows is called a gulp.

Collared Dove

These grey-brown birds have white tail feathers and dark wing-tips. Their eyes are deep red. Their name comes from the black half-collars on the backs of their necks. They like to nest near houses. Collared doves live in groups called dules.

European Starling

The dark, spotted feathers of starlings shimmer purplish-green in the light. Their beaks are dark in winter, but turn yellow in spring when looking for a mate. Instead of cawing calls, they whistle and rattle, and are very good at copying the sounds of other birds. Starlings live in groups called murmurations.

Crow

These large black birds can be seen perched at the tops of trees. They croak three or four times in a row, as a hello to the fairies. They are intelligent and can trick other birds to steal their food. They will eat almost anything. Crows live in groups called murders.

Barn Owl

If your garden backs onto open countryside, then you might see a barn owl. These large birds have white, heart-shaped faces and black piercing eyes. Their long, brown wings allow them to fly silently when hunting, earning them the nickname ghost owls. They have long talons and powerful beaks.

Ready for Nesting

Early springtime is hard for birds, as food is still scarce and they're trying to build nests and raise chicks. Here are some things you can do to help them.

1 Hair makes great nesting material for birds. When you brush your hair (or your dog's or cat's), ball up the little strands left on the brush and peg them to the washing line.

2 Scatter birdseed in your garden every morning. When it is really cold, you could also hang a fat ball from a branch to attract greenfinches and house sparrows.

3 Put up a bird box ready for nesting season. You can buy one from a garden centre, or make your own.

4 If the ground is frosty, water can be scarce, so you can help by making a bird bath. Find a shallow container such as an old dustbin lid. Put some rocks in it for the birds to stand on, and place it on four bricks laid out in a square. Change the water every day or two to prevent disease.

5 Finally, keep an eye on the number of birds coming into the garden. If you make it a haven for them, they will reward you later with the sight of baby birds leaving the nest and learning to fly.

Welcome, Feathered Friends

1
Cut a 2-3 cm hole a third of way up the side of the bottle.

You only need a few things to make a simple bird feeder for your garden:
- a plastic bottle • string
- scissors • two wooden spoons
- birdseed • an adult to help

2
Put the handle of a wooden spoon into the hole, until it hits the other side. Cut a small hole there, just big enough for the spoon handle to fit through.

3
Repeat steps one and two nearer to the top of the bottle.

4
Tie a long piece of string around the top of the bottle, so you can hang the feeder.

5
Carefully fill your bottle with birdseed and put the lid on.

6
Ask an adult to help you hang your brand new bird feeder high up, away from wind and rain.

7
Enjoy watching hungry birds feast on seeds. Just remember to keep it topped up!

Sun-kissed Summer Days

Summer brings with it leaves in every shade of green and a rainbow of flowers. Rosebuds start to open and sunflowers, encouraged by the fairies, begin to creep up, taller and taller. As the weather turns warmer, fairies coax the garden's harvest to grow. Raspberries and strawberries slowly ripen into beautiful reds and pinks, ready for picking.

Warm, hazy days beckon squirrel kits out of their nests for the first time, and balmy nights invite bats to spread their wings. Birds seem louder and their song livelier as chicks step out onto the branches. Bees and insects begin to buzz about the open flowers, sipping on nectar and collecting pollen to take back to the hive. Long summer evenings allow you to enjoy the peaceful sounds of wildlife in your garden and the chance to see a fairy working through the night.

Garden Trees

Finders are great at being able to identify the trees growing in their gardens. Can you identify any of these trees in your garden using only their descriptions?

Tulip

The tulip tree has brown bark with deep grooves. Its flowers resemble tulips and smell faintly of cucumbers. Its leaves have four points, smooth edges and are almost rectangular.

Sweet Chestnut

The bark of the sweet chestnut tree is dark brown. The fairies make swirling grooves in the trunk as they climb up, looking for sweet chestnuts. The dark, yellowish leaves are oblong and have serrated edges. They feel leathery, which is a side-effect of fairy magic.

Walnut

The brown-grey bark of the walnut tree has deep grooves which make excellent slides for playful fairies. In autumn, it produces walnuts inside thick green capsules, which turn brown and fall to the ground when ripe. It has long, oval leaves, with smooth edges.

Tibetan Cherry

The coppery-brown, peeling bark of the Tibetan cherry tree makes it very recognisable. It doesn't grow very tall, but it is very popular for its pinkish-white flowers that appear around May. Its leaves are small, long and have serrated edges.

Himalayan Birch

This tall tree has a white, papery bark. It's a nice snack for aphids and sawflies, who are regularly asked by fairies to stop ravaging the leaves. The leaves are wide at the bottom and pointed towards the top, with serrated edges. Unusually, they feel hairy when touched.

Red Maple

The red maple tree has dark brown bark. The seeds are called samaras or "helicopters". When they fall from the tree, they spin and twirl, mimicking the fairies who look after them. Their leaves have five sections, each ending in a point, and serrated edges.

Night Blooming Flowers

Some flowers only bloom when the moon is bright, blanketing the garden in a silvery glow. Fairies work their careful magic on these flowers, encouraging them to open and fill the dark garden with unique scents.

Nottingham Catchflies

These pink and white flowers bloom between May and July. Their leaves are covered in soft hairs and their sweet smell attracts pollinators, such as insects and bees. They are a favourite of the fairies, but they take a lot of magic to grow, which is why each flower only opens for three nights a year.

Common Evening Primrose

The four yellow petals of this flower hide a magical secret: each has a pattern on it, drawn by fairies, that is invisible to human eyes. It can bee seen by moths and guides them towards the nectar.

Four O'clocks

These flowers last only one night before wilting. As the flower ages, the night fairies change its colour from yellow to pink, or white to violet.

Night-scented Stock

During the day these pastel flowers look wilted, but at twilight they open and release a spicy vanilla fragrance that makes them very attractive to moths and butterflies. The fairies love the smell so much that they keep them growing from early April to late June.

FAIRY FAVOURITE:
Orange Jumpers

The rare orange jumper flower is named because its petals look like tiny, upside-down jumpers. It blooms for just one hour, right before sunrise, and it is how the fairies know that night-time is ending. By the time the sun is up, the flower is gone.

How Seeds Grow

Every gardener know that seeds are the first step to growing beautiful plants. But do you know how the magic happens?

Most plants grow from seeds. The tough outer coating protects the seed inside, which holds all the information for creating a new plant.

Seeds can lie dormant for years before they germinate (start to grow). Water, air and warmth encourage the seed to split open and send out a tiny root. The root sucks up water from the ground.

Next, the seed sends out a shoot which sprouts two little leaves. The leaves absorb sunlight and carbon dioxide from the air, which the plant uses to make food.

When the plant is fully grown, it sends out buds that open into flowers. Helpful insects, like bees, spread a special dust called pollen from flower to flower. The pollen makes flowers produce new seeds.

The flower's last job is to spread out its seeds. They fall out of the flower's head and are carried away by wind, water, animals or helpful gardeners.

Are There Bats in Your Garden?

Have you ever seen a dark shape swooping over your garden?
You might have been lucky enough to have seen a bat.

- When flying, bats can turn sharply, reverse suddenly and twist around street lights. Most birds can't do this.

- Most bats can't walk, but most birds can. Birds will push off from trees with their claws, whereas bats will hang upside and fall into flight.

- Bats are slower than most small garden birds, because they don't have hollow bones, which means they are heavier for their size.

- Bats have fingers and can bend them so that it looks like they're crumpling their wings in flight.

Building a Bat Haven

Do you have an old, hollow tree, or tumble-down building in your garden? These are the most popular spaces for bats to roost, so you're more likely to see them. Just don't get too close! Bats are a protected species and disturbing them is a crime.

Is your garden lit up like a sports stadium? Bats are put off by bright lights, especially if they're pointing directly into trees. Turn down your lights or point them away from places where bats might roost.

Are your plants and flowers attracting a bat banquet? Flowers such as daisies and lilies attract a lot of insects, which the bats will swoop down to catch. Little herb gardens and pond plants will do the same.

Did you know that a single bat can eat up to 3,000 insects in just one night?

The Fairy Postal Express

During the summer, there is a secret way to contact the fairies: the Fairy Postal Express. You don't need a stamp, an envelope or a post box. All you need is a piece of paper, a dandelion and something to say.

Use the sap in the stem of the dandelion to write your message on the paper. It will be hard to read and almost invisible, but don't worry, the fairies will know what it says.

Once you've finished with your note, leave it in a warm, sunny spot. In a day or two, go back to it and, if the invisible words have magically appeared, the fairies have read your message.

Just don't expect a reply: fairies can't write.

Fairy Song Catchers

As they work, fairies sing to make each other happy. Their song also has magical properties: it lets the flowers and wildlife in the garden know too that autumn is coming. Finders are more attuned to the song than most humans. However, even the best Finder needs help to gather the song. This is where a song catcher is useful. It can collect the fairy magic and, when the wind blows, release the song back into the garden.

1 Collect five twigs of similar size to make the top of your catcher. Wood from different types of trees will make the magic stronger.

2 Tie your twigs together into a star shape. Try and use only things you find in your garden, such as long grass or reeds.

When the wind releases the song from the catcher...

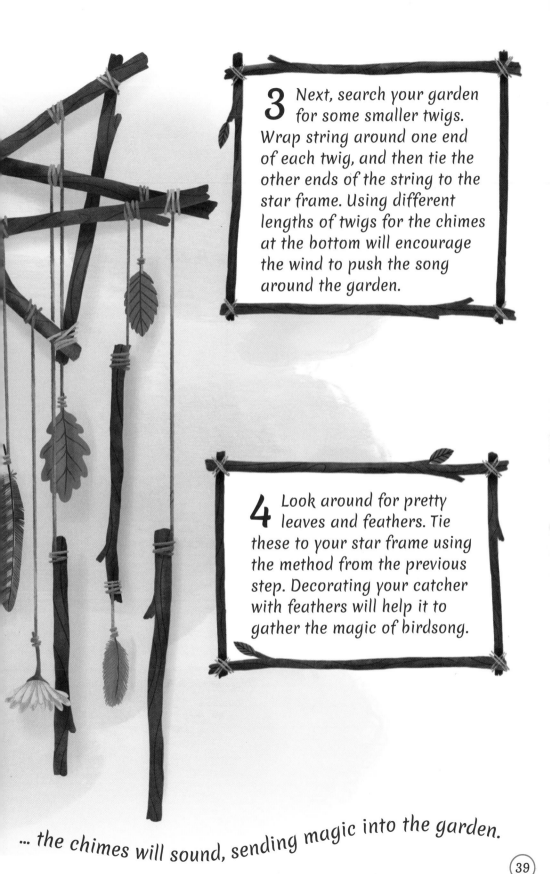

3 Next, search your garden for some smaller twigs. Wrap string around one end of each twig, and then tie the other ends of the string to the star frame. Using different lengths of twigs for the chimes at the bottom will encourage the wind to push the song around the garden.

4 Look around for pretty leaves and feathers. Tie these to your star frame using the method from the previous step. Decorating your catcher with feathers will help it to gather the magic of birdsong.

... the chimes will sound, sending magic into the garden.

The Golden Glow of Autumn

As mornings grow colder and the sun stays lower
in the sky, summer fades away and autumn, bursting
with colour, takes its place. Leaves turn from green
to yellow, orange and finally brilliant red. These fiery
displays are fleeting and the leaves soon fall from
the branches. This transformation brings juicy
blackberries bursting ready for tasting.

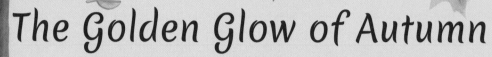

Can you spot the signs of wildlife preparing for winter?
Birds readying to migrate south to warmer climates,
or hunting for somewhere cosy to rest. Fairies helping
squirrels look for food to fill their winter stashes.
Spiders spinning intricate webs under loose bark
where they will be protected from the cold.

Beautiful Butterflies

On warm days in early autumn, the last butterflies of the year can be seen fluttering around the late flowers, feeding on nectar. On a warm day, sit in your garden and have a go at identifying these beautiful butterflies.

Comma

The comma gets its name from a small, white marking on its underside, which looks like a comma. When its wings are closed, its jagged outline makes it look like a withered leaf. The comma then becomes almost invisible when resting on a tree trunk or during hibernation.

Painted Lady

The forewings of a painted lady are orange with black tips and white spots. The hindwings have rows of black spots. The undersides are pale with blue eyespots. They cannot survive the cold winter so, at the end of autumn, they migrate to Africa.

Red Admiral

With its velvety black and red wings, the red admiral flutters around flowers, looking for sweet nectar. The caterpillars of these butterflies feed on stinging nettles.

Small White

The small white has white, veiny wings, with small black tips and one or two spots. The undersides of the wings are creamy white. They lay their eggs on cabbages and will often seek them out. They prefer the nectar of white flowers.

FAIRY FAVOURITE:
Glassy Patch

The blue and purple patchwork butterfly is an amazing sight. Their pointy wings have see-through patches, similar to stained glass. They are very rare and will only eat nectar from the flowers of the golden fae berry bush.

Scavenger Hunt

Early autumn nights are the perfect time to sit and admire the fairies' hard work. What can you see? What can you hear? Can you see the glow of the fairies at work?

Can you hear the call of a nearby owl saying hello to a fairy?

Can you spot a spider scuttling up a tree?

Can you see the glimmer of fireflies dancing with the fairies?

Can you hear the high-pitched chirping of crickets?

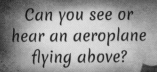

Can you see or
hear an aeroplane
flying above?

Can you see a spider's
web glistening in the
moonlight?

Can you hear the
rustling of leaves
in the breeze?

Can you see a
frog, hopping through
the bushes, looking for a
place to spend winter?

Can you see a
fluttering moth?

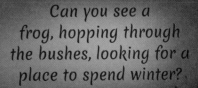

Common Garden Fruits

Throughout summer all sorts of fruits have been ripening through the summer, and now in autumn, they are finally ready. Many of them are a tasty snack for birds and animals, as well as for fairies and humans. How many can you spot in your garden?

 Warning: do not eat any berries unless an adult has told you that they're safe.

Raspberries

These dark pink berries are full of sweet tasting juice. They are very delicate, so be gentle when trying to take them off the bush. The flowers of these berries are loved by bees, who flock to the nectar they produce.

Apples

There are over 7,500 different varieties of apple and they can be any shade of green, yellow, pink or red. Some apples are sweeter than others. The tart ones are usually used for cooking.

Blackberries

These blue-black fruits are everywhere in autumn They look similar in shape to raspberries, but they are darker and slightly bigger. Going blackberry picking is a great way to spend an afternoon in autumn, but be careful of the thorns.

Cherries

Sweetest when their skins are a dark, plump red, cherries normally grow in pairs. In the centre of each fruit is a round, hard stone, which is actually a seed.

FAIRY FAVOURITE:
Golden Fae Berries

Brilliant gold in colour, these round berries are the size of blueberries. They have a super sweet taste and fairies use them in lots of their food. However, they are only edible on one day each year.

1

A lot of butterflies feed on fallen fruits and berries. Put some mushy bananas or ripe mangos out for them to feast on.

2

Butterfly houses are a great way to give butterflies and moths somewhere to rest during the winter. They can be purchased from garden centres.

Six
Ways to Help Butterflies and Moths in Autumn

3

Don't tidy up the garden before autumn. Caterpillars might attach themselves to dried flower stems and grasses when they turn into a chrysalis.

4

Should you find a butterfly in your house, move it some place cool. Carefully catch it in a box, and take it to an unheated building. Leave the lid open so the butterfly can fly away in spring.

5

Let stinging grow. They might be a pain to us, but butterfly larvae feed on the leaves during the spring and moths feed on them during autumn, when food is scarce.

6

If you've got space, plant some ivy. Ivy flowers in late autumn, and gives moths a supply of nectar when the weather is colder.

A Moth's Midnight Feast

The delicate patterns on their soft wings make moths a magical sight to see. They are attracted to the scents of flowers and to bright lights. Bring the moths to you by making a little midnight feast for them to enjoy. It's quicker than waiting for a moth to fly past your face.

You will need: • 50g black treacle • 100g brown sugar • 50ml fizzy cola • a paintbrush • an adult to help

1 Ask an adult to heat the cola in a large pan and let it simmer for 3 minutes. Do not bring it to the boil.

2 Stir in the sugar and treacle, and simmer for 2 more minutes.

3 Allow the mixture to cool down before putting it into a container.

4 Paint some of the mixture onto a couple of tree trunks or fence posts just before dusk.

5 Moths will be attracted to the sweet smell and taste of the mixture, so grab a torch and watch!

Night Fliers

Learn to identify different moths by looking at the patterns on their wings. Remember, you will only see some moths at certain times of the year.

Cinnabar Moth

Caterpillars of the cinnabar moth love to eat their way through patches of ragwort. The bright colours on the wings of the butterfly tell predators that they do not taste nice. All that ragwort has made them poisonous.

Lime Hawk-moth

The wings of the lime hawk-moth act as camouflage, allowing them to hide from predators. They only fly on warm evenings. As their name suggests, these moths can be found on lime trees.

Leopard Moth

It's not just the wings of the leopard moth that are spotted: their legs are black and white, too. The adults cannot feed and only live for eight to ten days each summer. They spend their short lives laying eggs.

Garden Tiger Moth

The garden tiger moth has a fascinating talent: it can squeak to warn bats in the area to stay away. This is a good thing, as these moths are rather poisonous, even to humans. Fairies, however, are immune to their poison and these fascinating moths help the fairies move from one flower to another.

Argent and Sable Moth

Argent and sable moths are rare visitors to gardens, so you should feel very lucky if you see one. Their name means silver (argent) and black (sable). The fairies taught these clever creatures to "spin" together a pair of leaves and make a little tent, where they can feed, grow and hide from predators.

Magpie Moth

By now you might be able to guess what the bright yellow and black spots on this moth are for: to warn predators that they are poisonous and not for eating.

FAIRY FAVOURITE:
Purple Herald Moth

During the day, these moths sleep under the leaves of the cloudy starwort flower. But as night falls, they spread their large, purple and gold wings to carry out important work for the fairies.

Wonderful Wormery

Earthworms can turn garden waste, like dead leaves and apple cores, into nutrients, which plants take up through their roots to help them grow. This makes the fairies very happy.

Build your own worm home using a jar. Poke some holes in the lid and put it in a cool, dark place when you've finished.

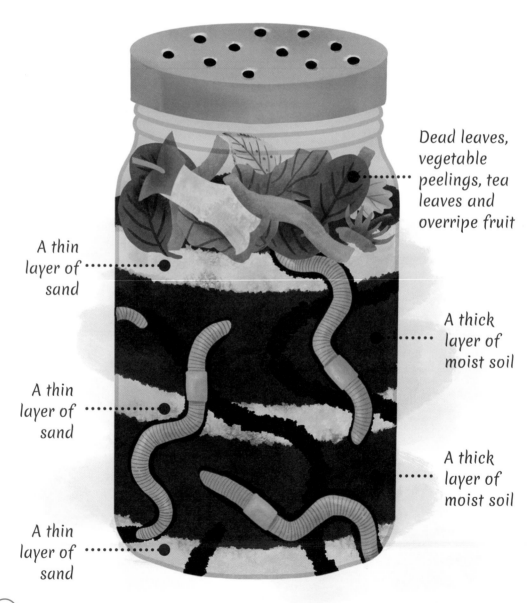

Dead leaves, vegetable peelings, tea leaves and overripe fruit

A thin layer of sand

A thin layer of sand

A thin layer of sand

A thick layer of moist soil

A thick layer of moist soil

Tips

Try not to handle the earthworms too much as the salt on your skin is toxic to them, dehydrating them quickly. It is why they wiggle so much when picked up.

Do not put citrus fruits or onions in your jar. They make the soil more acidic which can kill earthworms.

Observations

As the worms wiggle around under the soil, they mix the layers and the broken down plants together. This nutrient-rich soil is great for plants.

You could set up two jars, one with earthworms and the other with tiger worms. See which ones are hungrier. Don't mix them in the same jar, however, as they behave differently.

Following Footprints

A number of creatures will pass through your garden throughout the year. They leave evidence behind in the form of their tracks. Develop your Finder skills by studying footprints left behind in mud or snow.

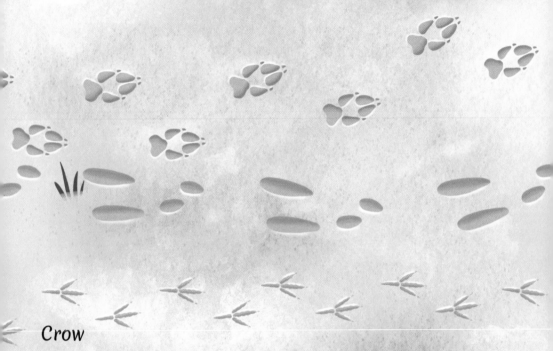

Crow

Crow footprints are quite large. Because crows are a ground-dwelling species, they walk instead of hopping, their prints alternate and turn slightly inwards, similar to human footprints.

Fairy

Fairy footprints will be shaped like yours, but much, much tinier. The tracks might start and end suddenly, which indicates a fairy landing on the ground or taking off.

Red Fox

The tracks of the red fox look similar to those of a dog, but narrower. While most dogs run around in circles chasing their tails, foxes tend to travel in straight lines as it is more efficient.

Rabbit

Because rabbits hop, all four of their prints are set closely together. Their hind feet are much larger than their forefeet, so there are two short prints at the front and two longer towards the back. Rabbits are very social animals, so you might see multiple sets of tracks.

Dog

If you have a dog or cat, it's a good idea to study their footprints so you don't confuse them with other animal prints.

The World of Minibeasts

Dark, damp corners are the perfect place to seek out minibeasts. Put a red filter such as a cellophane sweet wrapper over the end of your torch as that is less likely to scare insects away.

Woodlice

These dome-shaped creatures like to live in dark, damp places. When a woodlouse grows too big for its hard shell it has to get rid of it so a bigger shell can take its place. First the back half is shed and a day or two later the front half falls off.

Ladybirds

Ladybirds help gardens by eating bugs that nibble plants. There are 6,000 different species of ladybirds around the world. The most common species has seven spots. Look closely and try and count them.

Earwigs

Earwigs are never found in ears! They like to hide in little crevices and they don't do well in cold weather. They have small pincers on their stomachs. Earwigs also have wings, but most are reluctant to fly.

Garden Snails

The spirals on a snail's shell are called whorls, and there are usually four or five of them. A snail's mucus is so thick that they can slide over rocks without getting hurt. They sleep for up to 15 hours a day.

Black Garden Ants

These insects can live in colonies of between 4,000 and 7,000 ants. The queen ant can live for around 15 years. Ants like sweet food, and when one of them finds some, they make a scent trail so the others can follow. Some of the worker ants will carry food back to the colony.

Use your bug collecting box or a glass jar to get a closer look at some of the amazing and magical minibeasts in your garden. Be gentle when handling them and put them back where you found them.

Can you tell how they move?   How many legs do they have?

What markings can you see?   Can you see their eyes?

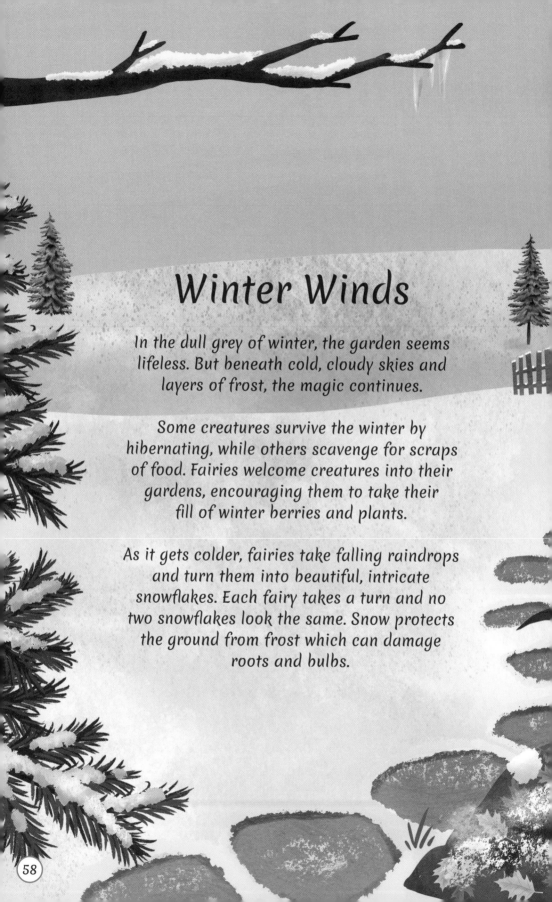

Winter Winds

In the dull grey of winter, the garden seems lifeless. But beneath cold, cloudy skies and layers of frost, the magic continues.

Some creatures survive the winter by hibernating, while others scavenge for scraps of food. Fairies welcome creatures into their gardens, encouraging them to take their fill of winter berries and plants.

As it gets colder, fairies take falling raindrops and turn them into beautiful, intricate snowflakes. Each fairy takes a turn and no two snowflakes look the same. Snow protects the ground from frost which can damage roots and bulbs.

Winter Wildlife Sanctuaries

Winter is hard on wildlife. Some animals struggle to find a home for the winter. Learn how to make simple homes for these important guests. It will give the fairies time to help other wildlife.

Male frogs go to the bottom of the pond, but female frogs hibernate on land. Dig a small hole, about 10 cm deep and 15 cm wide, near the pond. Place some gravel, twigs and dead leaves in the hole. Find a flat stone or piece of slate and place it over the hole. Leave a frog-sized gap so they can get in! In spring the fairies will visit them to let them know it's time to wake up.

Find an old wooden crate or plastic box to build a hide. If you use a plastic box, cut a door, just big enough for the hedgehog. Put it in a quiet corner of your garden, out of the way of wind or rain, and cover it in soil. Add a layer of dead leaves and twigs inside. Sometimes a fairy will go inside and have a nap next to a warm hedgehog.

Frogs

Hedgehogs

Turn over for tips on building bug hotels!

We need to help the fairies look after bees throughout the winter. Bumblebees live together in colonies, so find an old teapot with a lid. Dig a hole in the soil and bury the teapot, leaving only the spout sticking out. Bumblebees will use the spout to get in and out. Solitary bees live on their own. Bundle up a handful of bamboo canes or paper straws and tie them to a branch using string. Tie them tightly and somewhere away from the wind and rain.

As it turns colder, you might see a wood mouse looking for scraps. Build them a home by gathering some straw, twigs and logs. Find a corner of the garden and pile up the logs and twigs, leaving a couple of tiny, fist size gaps in between. This might take a few tries, but keep building it up again until you think it's right. Fill the gaps with straw for warmth. Continue piling logs and twigs on top to make a roof. The fairies will make sure the wood mice are safe and warm.

Bumblebees and Solitary Bees

Wood Mice

Bug Hotels

Minibeasts do a lot to help our gardens. Help them during the winter by building a bug hotel. You can buy them in garden centres, or make your own by filling an old bird box. Use these tips to decide what bug nesting material to use.

A slanted roof is vital so that rain runs off instead of sitting on the roof.

Dry bark and rotting wood provide a fantastic place for centipedes, woodlice and beetles.

Don't paint, varnish or cover the hotel.

Cut the top off a plastic drinks bottle. Roll up some corrugated cardboard and put it inside the bottom of the bottle for lacewings to crawl in.

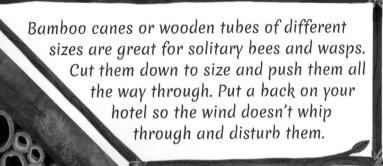

Bamboo canes or wooden tubes of different sizes are great for solitary bees and wasps. Cut them down to size and push them all the way through. Put a back on your hotel so the wind doesn't whip through and disturb them.

Ladybirds like to spend the winter surrounded by sticks and straw.

The hotel should be sheltered so that it doesn't get soaked every time it rains.

Dead leaves and dry twigs make the perfect shelter for ground beetles during winter.

Hidden Corners

In the darkest corner of the garden, where the ground is damp, there is a whole world of life to see. Mushrooms, lichens and moss come in all different shapes, colours and sizes, providing food and shelter to lots of creatures.

Warning: don't mess with mushrooms you don't know!

Velvet Shanks

These orange-capped mushrooms grow in clusters on rotting trees and wood. Their stems feel like velvet. They survive freezing temperatures, making them a popular food for animals and insects. The velvet shank mushroom has very poisonous lookalikes, so don't pick them.

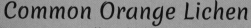

Common Orange Lichen

This orange-yellow lichen has very flat, overlapping leaves. In bright sunlight, it is orange, but in partial shade it can look greenish grey.

Wall Screw-moss

When dry, the leaves of this moss are twisted like screws, hence the name. It grows in little tufts and has very thin, silvery hair growing out of its green cushion.

Grey-cushioned Grimmia

This dark green moss has leaves that end in very fine hair points, making it look like it's growing long grey fur.

Scarlet Elf Cup

These cup-shaped mushrooms are usually found growing in little groups on dead wood. The insides of the cups are bright red. Fairies drink dew from inside the cups on chilly spring mornings, which boosts their flying ability.

Turkey Tail

Throughout the year, this flat, fan-shaped fungus grows in layered clusters on rotting logs or old tree stumps. The tough, leathery caps are usually brownish-red in colour. They were once used to decorate tables and hats.

65

Light the Way

The sun goes down much earlier in winter. As the dark starts to creep in, the fairies have to work to protect the flowers and creatures from the cold. It's hard finding everything that needs their attention in the dark. You can help to light their way by making ice lanterns for your garden.

Why not make lots of ice lanterns that are different shapes and sizes?

You will need: • two small tubs of different sizes • cold water • pebbles or rocks • a freezer • a candle • an adult to help

1 Half fill the largest tub about three quarters full with water.

2 Put the pebbles or small rocks into the smaller tub and place it inside the larger one. The tub should float and not be touching the bottom of the larger one. If it does touch, remove a few pebbles.

3 Carefully put the tubs in your freezer, making sure to keep them level.

4 When the water has frozen solid, remove the ice from the tubs.

5 Take it out to the garden and place it where you think it will be most useful for the busy fairies.

6 Put a tea light or small candle inside and ask an adult to light it for you.

Winter Berries

When the trees are bare, winter berries become vital to wildlife. The fairies carefully nurture the berries so that they provide food all winter.

 Warning: do not eat any berries unless an adult has told you that they're safe.

Rosehips

Rosehips are fruit of wild rose plants. They are small, round and usually red-orange in colour, but they can sometimes be dark purple-black. Fairies use them to treat Fae Jumping Fever, a disease that causes fairies to hop in circles without stopping.

Hawthorn Berries

From the thorny twigs of the hawthorn bush dangle bundles of scarlet-coloured berries. A long time ago they were used as medicine. They are far too bitter for fairies, who avoid them at all costs.

Rowan Berries

These berries hang on the trees until January, making them a valuable source of winter food for wildlife. Humans have used them to make many things, including jelly, but they cannot be eaten raw. Fairies cannot eat rowan berries, even if they're cooked. They cause them to turn bright orange.

Holly berries

The holly berry and prickly leaves are used as decoration during winter celebrations. Whilst very popular with birds, holly berries are poisonous to humans and to a lot of pets. A single drop of holly berry juice is enough to knock out a fairy for an entire day.

FAIRY FAVOURITE:
Fleeting Frost Berries

On the coldest day of the year, these black and white berries "sing" to the fairies. The fairies use them to make tea, which helps them to keep working through the cold winter. They are not as common as the other berries, because they require a lot of magic to grow.

Send a Magical Invitation

Fairy doors connect the human world to the Realm of the Fae, home of all fairies. Every time someone places a little door in their garden, a new connection is made to this hidden world and a group of fairies will enter the garden for the first time.

Use things found in your garden to make the fairies happy!

Encourage fairies to come into your garden by making your own fairy doors and placing them at the bottom of trees, next to a wall or even on the side of flower pots. They can be any shape, size, colour or style – the more imaginative the better.

Don't forget to add a door handle, so the fairies can get in!

Why not make two doors to invite more fairies into your garden?

A Finder's Notebook

Use these pages to keep a record of the things you find on your explorations. You could take notes of all that you hear, take a rubbing of the rings of a fallen tree or press a flower between the pages. If you are lucky and keep very quiet, you may even be able to sketch a fairy at work.

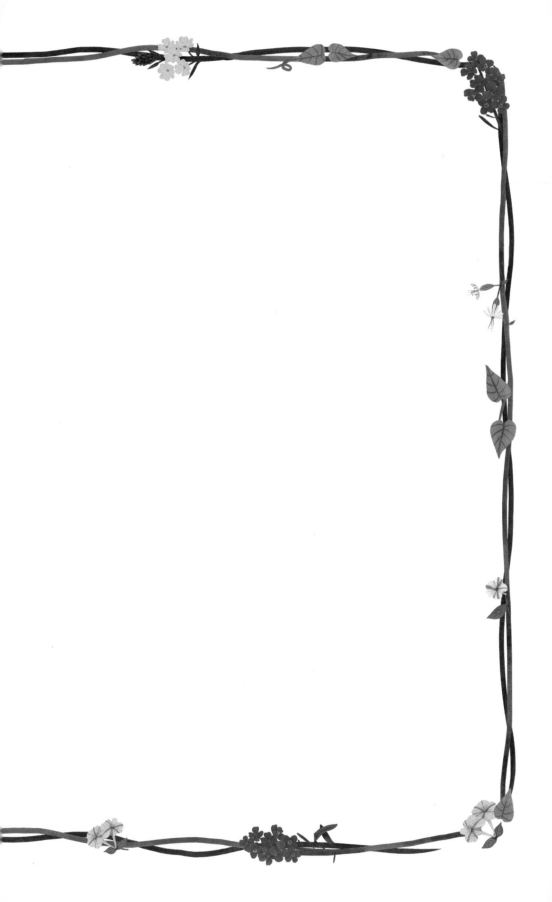

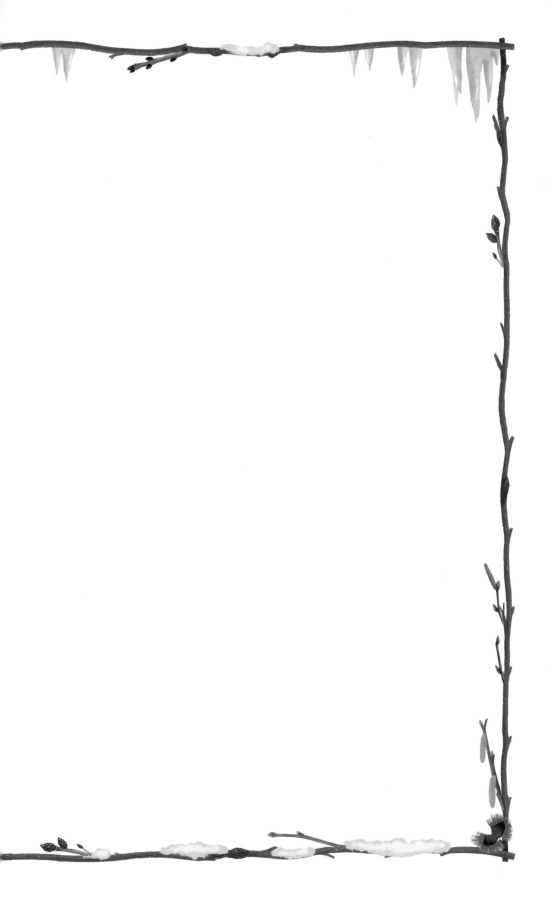

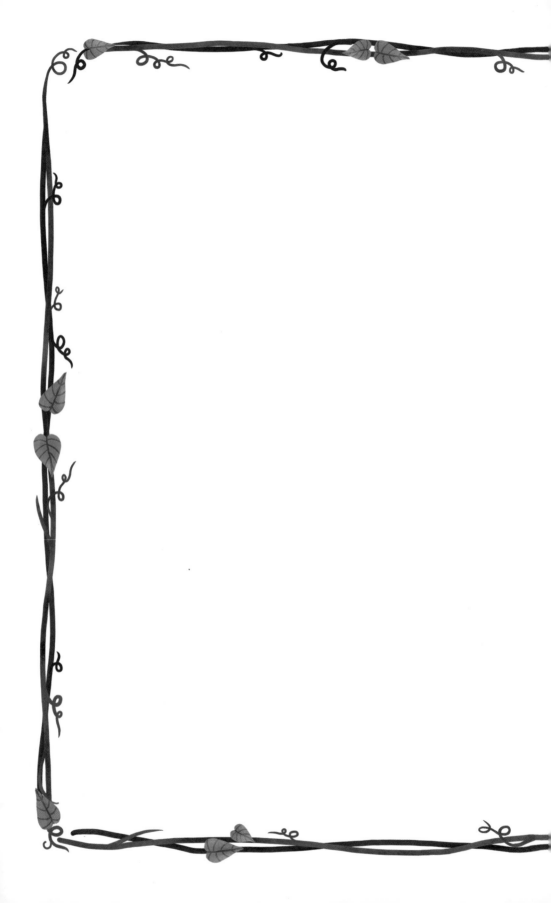

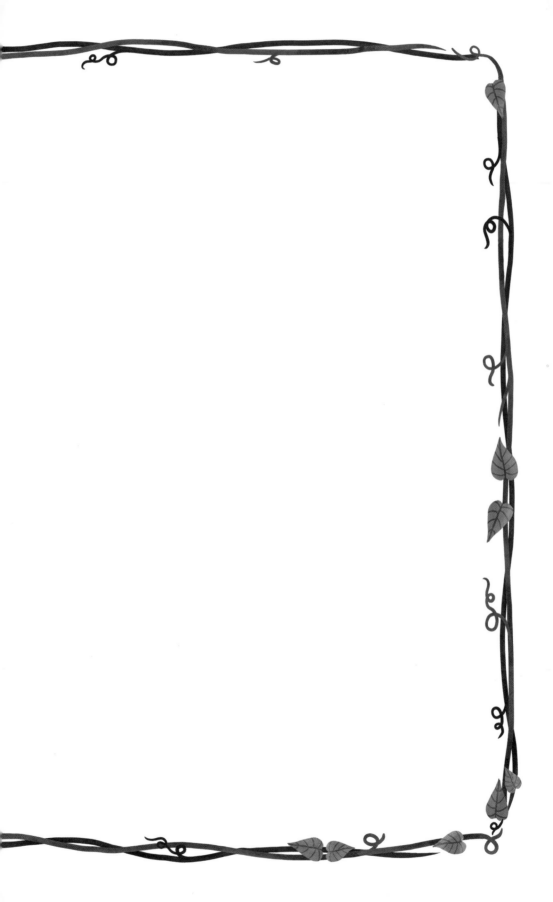

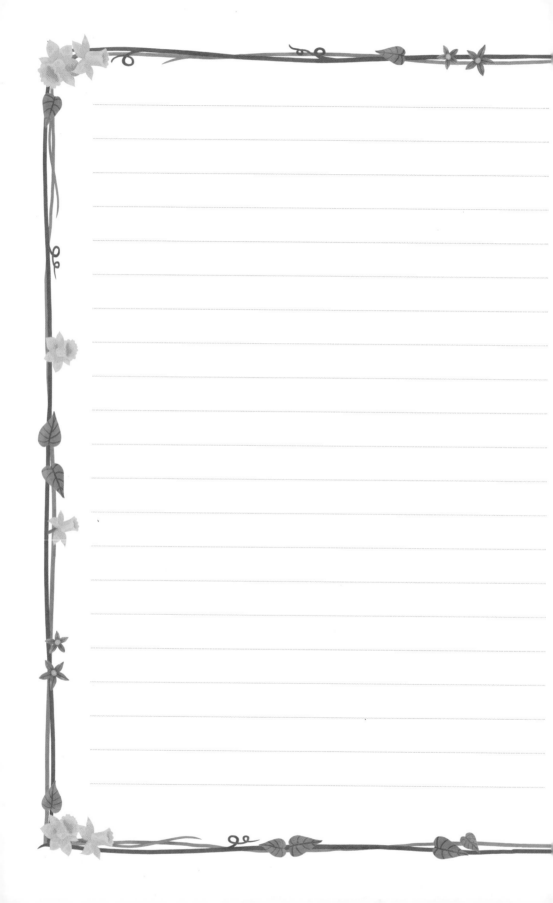

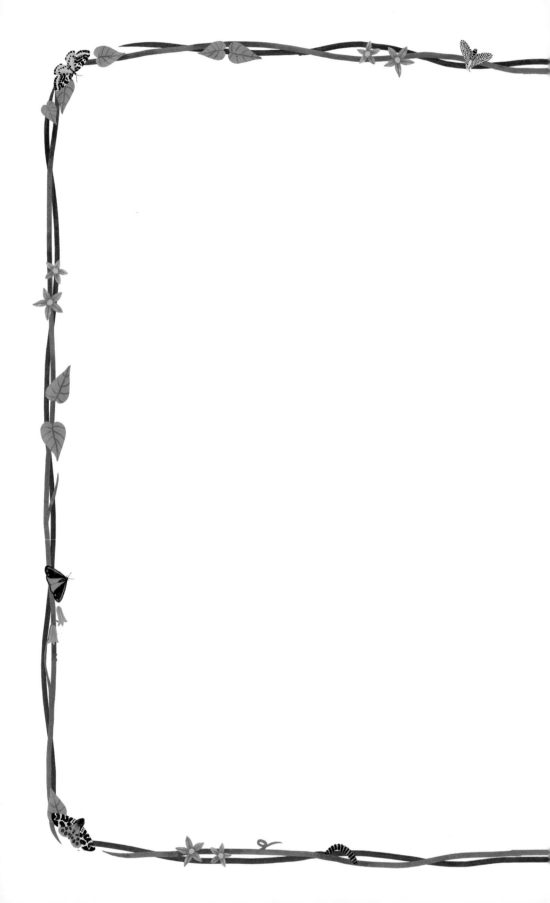

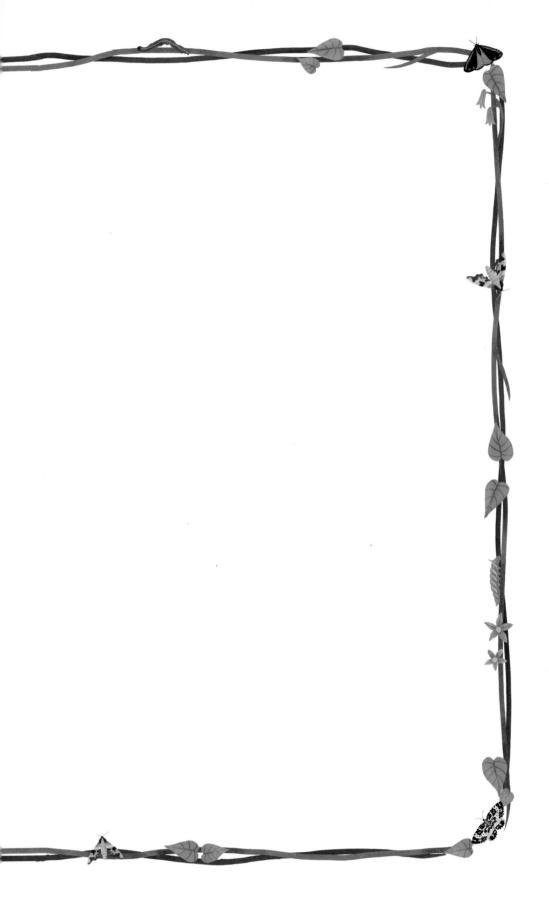

Index

A
animal sanctuaries 60-61
  bat havens 35
  bug hotels 62-63
  wormeries 52-53
ants 57
apples 46
argent and sable moths 51

B
backswimmers 20
barn owls 23
barn swallows 22
bats 34-35
bees 18-19, 61
berries
  autumn 46-47
  winter 68-69
birch trees 29
birds 22-23
  feeders 25
  nests 24
  tracks 54
black garden ants 57
blackberries 47
bug hotels 62-63
bug hunting 57
bumblebees 18-19, 61
butterflies 42-43
  in autumn 48

C
catchfly flowers 30
cherries 47
cherry trees 29
chestnut trees 28
cinnabar moths 50
cloudy starwort flowers 15
collared doves 22
comma butterflies 42
common blue damselflies 20
common evening primroses 30
common orange lichen 64
crickets 44
crocuses 14
crows 23, 54

D
daffodils 15
damselflies 20
dogs 55
doves 22
dragonflies 20
duckweed 21

E
earthworms 52-53
earwigs 56
eggs shells 16-17
European starlings 23
evening primroses 30

F
fairies
  doors 70-71
  finders kit 9, 10-11
  footprints 54
  song catchers 38-39

feeders
  bird 25
  moth 49
fireflies 44
fleeting frost berries 68
flowers 30-31, 33
footprints 54-55
four o'clock flowers 31
four-spotted chasers 20
foxes 55
frogs 45, 60
  tadpoles 21
fruits
  autumn 46-47
  winter 68-69

G
garden tiger moths 51
glassy patch butterflies 43
golden fae berries 47
golden snails 57
grey-cushioned grimmia 65

H
hawk-moths 50
hawthorn berries 68
hedgehogs 60
Himalayan birch trees 29
holly berries 68
honeybees 19
house sparrows 22
hunting
  bugs 57
  scavenger 44-45

I
insects 56, 57
  pond 20, 21
irises 15

L
ladybirds 56
lanterns 66-67
leopard moths 50
lichen 64
lights 66-67
lime hawk-moths 50

M
magpie moths 51
maple trees 29
mice 61
minibeasts 56-57
  bug hotels 62-63
  pond 20, 21
moss 65
moths 45, 50-51
  in autumn 48
  feeders 49
mushrooms 64, 65

N
nests
  bug hotels 62-63
night lights 66-67
night-blooming flowers 30-31
night-scented stocks 31
Nottingham catchfly flowers 30

O
orange jumper flowers 31
owls 23, 44

P
painted lady butterflies 42
plants 32-33
  flowers 30-31
  pots 16-17
pond skater 21
pond snails 21
ponds 20-21
primroses 30
purple herald moths 51

R
rabbits 55
raspberries 46
red admiral butterflies 43
red foxes 55
red maple trees 29
rosehips 68
rowan berries 68

S
scarlet elf cup mushrooms 65
scavenger hunts 44-45
screw-moss 65
seedlings 16-17, 32
seeds 32-33
  pots 16-17
skaters 21
small white butterflies 43
snails
  pond 21
  garden 57
snowdrops 14
sparrows 22
spiders 44, 45
starlings 23
stocks 31
swallows 22
sweet chestnut trees 28

T
tadpoles 21
Tibetan cherry trees 29
  tracks 54-55
trees 28-29
tulip trees 28
turkey tail fungus 65

V
velvet shank mushrooms 64

W
wall screw-moss 65
walnut trees 28
wasps 19
webs 45
wildlife sanctuaries 60-61
  bat havens 35
  bug hotels 62-63
  wormeries 52-53
wind chimes 38-39
wood mice 61
woodlice 56
wormeries 52-53